I pledge allegiance
Prometo lealtad

to the flag
a la bandera

under God,
ante Dios,

indivisible,

indivisible,

with liberty
con libertad

and justice
y justicia

for all.
para todos.

I pledge allegiance to the flag of the United States of America and to the Republic for which it stands, one Nation under God, indivisible, with liberty and justice for all.

Prometo lealtad a la bandera de los Estados Unidos de América y a la República a la que representa, una Nación ante Dios, indivisible, con libertad y justicia para todos.

one Nation
una Nación

for which it stands,
a la que representa,

and to the Republic
y a la República

of the United States of America
de los Estados Unidos de América

THE PLEDGE OF ALLEGIANCE
PROMESA DE LEALTAD

SCHOLASTIC INC.

New York   Toronto London Auckland Sydney
Mexico City   New Delhi   Hong Kong   Buenos Aires

Photography credits for *The Pledge of Allegiance*:
Cover: John Fleck/Stone; Back Cover: Art Montes De Oca/FPG; page 3: Chip Henderson/Stone;
page 4: SuperStock; page 5, top left: Chromosohn/Photo Researchers, right: Philip Spears/FPG, bottom left: Steve Skjold/PhotoEdit;
page 6, top left: Toyohiro Yamada/FPG, top right: Dennis Flaherty/Photo Researchers, bottom right: FPG, bottom left: SuperStock;
page 7: Harvey Lloyd/FPG; page 8: Paul Sakuma/AP Wide World Photo; page 9: Owen Franken/Corbis; page 10: NASA/AP Wide World Photo;
page 11, top left: Jerry Alexander/Stone, right: Peter Gridley/FPG, bottom left: SuperStock; page 12: PhotoDisc; page 13: Robert W. Ginn/PhotoEdit;
pages 14-15: Art Montes De Oca/FPG; page 16, left: SuperStock; pages 16-17: Arthur Tilley/FPG; page 18, background: David Young Wolff/PhotoEdit,
top left: Myrleen Ferguson Cate/PhotoEdit, right: Philip Spears/FPG, bottom left: Michelle & Tom Grimm/Stone; page 19: Art Montes De Oca/FPG;
page 20, left: Reza Estakhrian/Stone; pages 20-21: SuperStock; page 22: FPG; page 23: Michael Newman/PhotoEdit; page 24: FPG.

ISBN 0-439-31738-X

12 11 10 9 8 7 6 5 4 3 2 1   1 2 3 4 5 6/0

Printed in the U.S.A.   08

First Scholastic Bilingual printing, September 2001